Frictionless Motion

Derek Dohren

Black Eyes Publishing UK

Frictionless Motion
By Derek Dohren
© Derek Dohren, 2023

First published in 2023
Black Eyes Publishing UK
34 Stocken Close
Hucclecote, Gloucester
GL3 3UL (UK)

www.blackeyespublishinguk.co.uk

ISBN: 978-1-913195-24-3

Derek Dohren has asserted his moral right under the Copyright, Designs and Patents Act, 1988, to be identified as the author of this work.

All Rights reserved. No part of this publication may be reproduced, copied, stored in a retrieval system, or transmitted, in any form or by any means, without the prior written consent of the copyright holder, nor be otherwise circulated in any form of binding or cover other than that in which it is published and without a similar condition being imposed on the subsequent purchaser.

A CIP catalogue record for this title is available from the British Library.

Edited by: Josephine Lay

Cover illustration: From an original painting, 'At the Barranco de Huenes', by Derek Dohren

Cover design: Jason Conway, The Daydream Academy.
www.thedaydreamacademy.com

For my friend Ana,
busy exploring new worlds

in frictionless motion.

Introduction

As life experiences go, few can be quite as unsettling as being schooled by someone less than half your age. Sure, while I can gratefully accept a millennial demonstrating a phone app to me, or easily appreciate the skill of a talented music teacher patiently placing my fingers on a guitar fretboard there are certain areas of expertise to which one may assume age alone confers a superior wisdom. This is not necessarily so, of course.

I met Ana in 2010 in the beautiful Andalucian city of Granada. I was in the midst of an emotional crisis, inexplicably living in a foreign land, teaching English as a Second Language. Ana was from the island of Lanzarote and was studying languages at Granada's university. We hit it off immediately and it quickly became apparent the teacher/student relationship we had was a two-way street. I advised Ana on her already very good English and she set me on track to putting my life back together by restoring my confidence and self-belief. Our relationship wasn't always rosy. She was often infuriating, and I'm quite sure that was also reciprocal. In essence, we had problems the other was able to help with, but we had aspects of our lives that were alien to one another. Often, our meetings would generate a mutual bemusement, but there was laughter and a sense of fun; there was affection and respect.

In 2017 I returned to the UK. My life changed radically once more. Ana and I stayed in contact though inevitably the physical distance between us consigned our relationship to memories of a precious shared past. It felt enough just to have had those experiences, to keep them in a box I could open from time to time. After all, life moves on. Another four years would pass before Ana came crashing unexpectedly into my world once more.

On my return to the UK, I trained as a bus driver, and in the summer of 2021, I relocated with my bus driving job to the Isle of Skye in Scotland. It had been a long-held dream of mine to live on the island, and certainly one I had talked about with Ana. She was an islander and understood the magic I felt about Skye. Ana had shared with me her dreams of travel too. She wanted to work abroad, see the world, and have her own adventures.

For various reasons the Hebridean relocation turned into a huge misadventure (I returned south to England in a matter of weeks) but one of the most difficult times I experienced came in late August. I woke one Saturday morning with an overwhelming feeling I was dying.

I had no clear symptoms other than I could sense my life force draining out of me. My mind was dulled and I was unable to leave my flat. I barely had the energy to get through the day. I retired early to bed, believing I might not ever wake up again. But before I shut my eyes, I read the sad news that Ana had died suddenly. At some level of being I immediately understood that her death must be connected to how I was feeling. There had been a soul connection between us. In the morning I woke with my health fully restored. I was shocked and saddened by Ana's passing but felt reassured that her spirit had moved on and she was now safe. I've no scientific evidence whatsoever to lead me to these conclusions, but I don't require any.

When I began to put together this collection, I rediscovered several poems that related directly to Ana and others that had been inspired by our relationship. These are now in the second section of this book, which is dedicated to her memory. I've always harboured a fascination for the metaphysical; since those events on Skye I've become increasingly preoccupied with exploring such themes.

Inevitably, this fascination has bled into my poetry and *Frictionless Motion* marks that change.

My dearest wish is that through these words Ana's spirit will reach corners of the world and fulfil dreams she wasn't able to realise during her short time on Earth. x

Derek Dohren   December 2022.

Motionless Friction

- 15 Motionless Friction
- 17 The Purpose of Life
- 18 Weather Girl Crush
- 19 The First Half of a World Cup Qualifier
- 21 Diversions Are in Place
- 24 Bus Lane a Go Go
- 25 For Margot
- 27 Crabwood Crop Circle, England, 2002
- 28 Seurat
- 29 Pluto
- 31 Waiting For the Gas Man
- 32 Ain't Nobody
- 33 Celestial Subterfuge
- 34 Punishment
- 35 Old World
- 36 The Day Before the Funeral
- 37 Music Man
- 39 Time Machine
- 41 Coffee Chain Hues
- 42 Never
- 44 Mea Culpa
- 45 Last Day
- 46 Town and Country Life
- 47 They Bled Gnarled Fingers Dry
- 48 Three Choirs Festival
- 49 The Chains of Dogma

Frictionless Motion

53 Skye
54 Portrait
55 Frictionless Motion
56 Leave Some Things
57 The Day You Died
58 Timelines
59 The Wristwatch
60 The Dark Side of the Moon
61 Meteor Showers
62 Willing Hands No More
64 This Life

69 Other Works by Derek Dohren
71 Testimonials
73 Crabwood crop circle (image)
74 The Wow! Signal (image)

Note: *The Dark Side of the Moon* first appeared in *Everything Rhymes with Orange*, ISBN-13 978-1913195038, published by *Black Eyes Publishing UK*, in 2019.

Motionless Friction

Motionless Friction

Time's not linear
I lived a future life.
Event horizon whirlpool
now risking spaghettification.
When my cup of tea is finished
I'll go scale Hadrian's Wall again
with a bucket full of frogspawn
so I can go and terraform Mars
in motionless friction.
The perfection of birdsong is noted
but I just don't know
if the space in my head
is habitable or inhabitable.

I'm annoying the neighbours
with a noisy kitchen blender.
I thought I'd thrown away
my only pair of scissors.
Just how do you decide
on a houseplant's gender?
Your honey sweet lips
and a laptop upon my knee.
I think I've matured with rage.
A photo of the family, minus me
but I just don't know
if the stuff of this world
is flammable or inflammable.

Steering wheel judder
hits at 45 miles per hour.
I didn't turn right into Monmouth
instead, I turned wrong
past rainbow-kissed flowers
but damn those springtime blizzards.

I have lost all my perspective
and I'm waving at Vincent's wheatfield
a masterpiece of creation
spied through my shattered windshield
but I just don't know
if the experience of life
is valuable or invaluable.

The Purpose of Life

Chaos theory at Gloucester Quays
is once again subverted
as down in the South China Seas
a typhoon is averted.
I reflect on this as my 12-ton bus
runs over a butterfly;
the real purpose of life for us
is in learning how to die.

Bolsheviks storming the Winter Palace.
Those grassy knolls of downtown Dallas.

Being human's a tough gig though
spent musing on life's events
ponder long and watch them grow
have they all been Heaven sent?
I reflect on this at the terminus
and again, as I cruise on by
the real purpose of life for us
is in learning how to die.

That failed trial with Crystal Palace.
Strictly Come Dancing with Shirley Ballas.

Weather Girl Crush

I've got a weather girl crush
the biggest since records began
thermal ridges upwelling
on her occluded front
I'm gonna flash flood
my waterspout's already swelling.

I've got a weather girl crush
the hottest since records began
a cyclonic rotation
tropical convergence zones
heavy risk of cyclones
stratospheric oscillation.

I've got a weather girl crush
the longest since records began
the forecast looks bleak
a tropical depression
some moisture advection
it's gonna get wetter next week.

I've got a weather girl crush
the wettest since records began
convective instability
my Jetstream's veered north
I'm gonna pour forth
with extremely high humidity.

The First Half of a World Cup Qualifier

I was staying in a lovely hotel
down Malvern way.
England were on the telly
in a World Cup qualifier.
By the time they'd done
the national anthems
laid a wreath
played the last post
swapped pennants
taken the knee
and paid further tributes to the dead

my mind had wandered.
England had reverted to a 3-4-3
but I was considering the decor.
I gawped at a triptych
of Malvern Priory
that hung upon the wall.
A cloud over the scene looked like
one of those nuclear bomb mushrooms
or perhaps it was
the smoke-plume jizz
of an ejaculating rocket

and I was immediately reminded
of billionaires in space
shooting for the stars
when most of us would simply prefer them
to be making honest tax returns.
Harry Maguire scored and cupped his ears
and knee-slid away all of the jeers.
I didn't know why
a fellow guest called Fran
had bored me with talk of antiques

she'd be flogging off
a lovely piece of Clarice Cliff
that her Frankie bought in Donetsk.
Harry Kane nodded in a second
from a Jordan Henderson cross
that was Trent Alexander Arnold-esque.
I had the sound turned off
and was gorging on the hotel Wi-Fi
experimenting with
Gregorian chants on Spotify

when Henderson made it three.
I'd told Fran I was a famous poet
and she said that she'd google me.
Now, Barber's Adagio for Strings
Raheem Sterling, Declan Rice
Tyrone Mings.
I'd never understood before why
people plan their own funerals.

Kane made it four
then he made it five.
A hat-trick before half time.

Diversions Are in Place

The B4224 at Lea is closed
for flood-defence work.

Diversions are in place.

Pull in to the bus stop at Lea Church
then reverse into Orchard View
return to the junction
of the B2244 and the B2422
and take the first left
for the B2244
continue down the B2244 to The Crown Inn
and turn right onto the B4244.
Continue to Longhope
and turn right at the Nags Head
to rejoin the B4224.

I receive an update.
The B2424 into Gloucester is closed
for pot-hole repair work.

Diversions are in place.

All traffic normally entering Gloucester
from the B2424
is to divert down the B4422.
Continue down the B4224
and turn left at the Red Lion
to join the B4422.
Continue on to Gloucester.

At Gloucester Transport hub
I'm unable to park in my allocated bay
because another bus is already there.

I divert to the adjacent slot
and annoy the driver coming in behind me
because I'm now in his bay
and he is forced to divert accordingly.
We acknowledge one another
and smile behind our masks
but quietly we are seething inside.

Before I leave the hub
I check for updates.

Sheep are on the road on the B2442.
There's a sink hole in Hoarwithy on the B4242
and subsidence in Sling on the B2224.
There are potatoes at Peterstow all across
the newly reopened section of the B4424.
There has been a landslide at Kerne Bridge
and the B4442 is closed.
BT are ripping up the pavements on the B2242.
Tree felling and hedge cutting is taking place
all along the B4244.

Expect delays.

And on the messages come.

A nuclear submarine has beached on the B2222.
Aliens have landed on the B4444.
A woolly mammoth has shit itself
outside the Dog and Muffler pub
in English Bicknor on the B2442
and that's why there are
temporary traffic lights in operation
at the junction of the B2444 and the B4222.

Diversions are in place.

I arrive back at Ross-on-Wye, 224 minutes late
and retire to the rest room.

I fish out a coin
and feed it into the vending machine
before
I see the post-it note that reads
"Machine fucked"
and I lose my 50p.

I smile behind my mask
but quietly I am seething inside.

Bus Lane a Go Go

I love driving down empty bus lanes
sometimes I feel like they're all mine
though I must stop doing it in my car
as I can't afford the sixty quid fine.

For Margot

I don't have to try too hard
to be something I already am.

I think I'll go for a walk
round my padded cell.
Go and bounce off a puzzling bedspread.
Winds wet with rain
from warmer climes.

Let me tell you that joke
about the Titanic.
It always goes down well.

I love the sight
of fresh cut grass
and the smell
of a sunrise over the moors.

Go and strangle a guzzling petrol pump.
I like to bring home stuff I find
from long country walks.
Sun gazing in Watford
while hiding in laughter
as hail pounds my roof.

Telekinesis is real
if you believe that sort of thing.
The neighbour's post
is in my mailbox again.

Go and massage a hillock of jelly babies.
I can't come out to play
I'm busy practising the didgeridoo.

Anne Frank's older sister Margot
also kept a diary.
It was never found.

Crabwood Crop Circle, England, 2002

See, they weave
their stalks
here and there.

"Beware the bearers of FALSE gifts
& their BROKEN PROMISES.
Much PAIN but still time.
BELIEVE."

As real as
the glass prism-splintered light
raining down
from blue skies.

"There is GOOD out there.
We OPpose DECEPTION.
Conduit CLOSING."

See, they weave
their stalks
from nowhere.

Note: *This crop circle appeared in a Wiltshire field on August 15th, 2002. It depicted an alien holding a CD which displayed a message coded in ASCII characters (translated into English in the poem).*

Crop circle enthusiasts have interpreted the message as emanating from an alien source. However, it was subsequently claimed the circle was created to generate publicity to promote the forthcoming Hollywood film 'Signs', starring Mel Gibson and Joaquin Phoenix.

Seurat

George-Pierre Seurat was an outlier
who devised the discipline of chromoluminarism
with daddy's money
a Have, not a Have-Not,
in Impressionist Paris
France.

He was a mathematically minded
scatter-brained genius
privilege does as privilege will
A Sunday Afternoon on the Island of La Grande Jatte
on the banks of the River Seine.

George-Pierre Seurat was an outlier
who explored the discipline of divisionism
with daddy's money
no Claude Monet
in Impressionist Paris
France.

He was an artistically sensitive
logical precisionist
privilege does as privilege will
The Bathers at Asnières
on the banks of the River Seine.

George-Pierre Seurat was an outlier
who explored the discipline of pointillism
with daddy's money
no Édouard Manet
in Impressionist Paris
France.

Pluto

Am I the frozen dwarf
or the God of the Underworld?
You decide.
Dark white
but not quite grey.
In my distracted distance
Renaissance awaits.
There is no cradle without a grave
no evolution of understanding
cryptic rhythms notwithstanding
of that which is truly arcane
acknowledging all that is usefully insane.

Release the chains of fear
the great revealer is here!
Frigid lost child of the Sun.
Who do you say that I am?
Everything as it used to be
or nothing the same as it was.
To the minimalist silver-tongued torturer
all art is self-portraiture.
Deconstructor of construction
in whose grip all die and become
swallowed in solar absolution.

Am I the frozen dwarf
or the God of the Underworld?
You decide.
Pale black
but not quite grey.
Do not be misled by size
for the microbe brings down the man.
I have my siblings lassoed.
The metamorphosis of circumstance

in elliptic mission circle dance
virtual reality broadcaster
and indiscriminate puppet master.

My eyes have all the measure
of submission and subjugation.
Keeper at the gates of delirium.
What does your heart speak of me?
Everything as it used to be
or nothing the same as it was.
Precision touchpad sorcerer
sacred geometry conjuror
instructor of instruction.
Stealer, healer of endings begun
the liberator of invention
re-wilding the tamed imagination!

Note: *This poem was commissioned to be written and performed at the Gustav Holst Museum in Cheltenham, in September 2018, as part of the centennial celebrations of Holst's Planet Suite.*

Waiting For the Gas Man

Waiting for the gas man,
think I'll listen to New Order.
Fixing up that painting
and drinking tea.
What else you gonna do
when you're waiting for the gas man?

Waiting for the gas man,
said he'd be here by now.
Rebooting my laptop
I need another tea.
What else you gonna do
when your day's not going to plan?

Waiting for the gas man,
still no sign of him yet.
Hanging up those clothes
best drink more tea.
What else you gonna do
when you don't see that white van?

Waiting for the gas man,
I'm gonna wash the dishes.
Watering my houseplants
I've run out of teabags.
What else you gonna do
when you're waiting for the gas man?

Ain't Nobody

Ain't nobody else here
just me and the tinnitus
and the tv has broken down
all I hold dear is illusion
hiding behind
the painted face of a clown.

Ain't nobody else hear
the sound of the ticking clock?
I can't even pick up the phone
and my coulrophobia is
my reality
masked by the face of a clone.

Celestial Subterfuge

It's not that there's no value in intimacy
and I can see why you may take comfort there
but best I just watch, like no one else is dancing
because I'm more of a caretaker, than a care giver.
Did you know there's something not right
about the planet Venus?
It's a tableau of stone in shattered shock.

Saturn's not what you think it is either.

Time flies but the sand falls slowly
so, if it's all the same to you
I'll be sticking to the shaded side of the pavement
plumbing the pre-pubescent undercurrents of life
while growing my sunflowers
behind closed doors.

There's no doubt real truth lies in fiction
where I prefer the catatonic, subatomic resonances.
I'm not one of those freewheeling jailbreakers
because honestly, honesty's not for the likes of me.
Did you know there are strange temperature anomalies
on the planet Neptune?
It's mindfully present, checking its body for ailments.

Evidence points to a past nuclear disaster on Mars.

I'm gazing at the Commonwealth war graves
fascination over the origins of life has nothing
to match my growing concern over how it all ends.
I'm nuzzling that Fat Man over Nagasaki,
trying to understand when biology
becomes chemistry.

Punishment

They spoke to her in vain
those voices from her past.
Those cocoas at bedtime had done nothing
for her daytime stress levels.

She angrily kicked a purple balloon
that, like her, had seen better days
removing the last vestige of her former self.
This was a place of punishment.

"Oxygen thieves", the warden had called them
excessively severe of temperament
yet someone always reserved enough puff
to blow up balloons.

People could be so devious
not unlike the mutton broth
served at dinnertime, as if to emphasise
this was a place of punishment.

Old World

Swanking down slippy, basalt stairs
unfixed in the eye of the beholder
I offered up my thoughts and prayers
rebuffing the chill of your cold shoulder.

It had been with some resistance
over moorland rock and heather
to that sodden brink of existence
our joyless feet had shed blood together.

That lump of Jurassic limestone
we used as a table and stool
you, clad in your classic rhinestone
me, squat in my lime green cagoule.

Sacred geometry omnipresent
a jingo bingo God fanatic
and oh, so sexy, yet unpleasant
a peripatetic glacial erratic.

But I feared both of us would lose
that ticking time-bomb two-horse race
rainbow showers don't make the news
when there's an old world fall from grace.

The Day Before the Funeral

Under pressure
cutting edge technology.
Men and women
with the expertise
and the latest techniques.
It's all about to kick off.

Episodes one to four
will be available on Catch-Up.
This is my lot now.
It really will be
the final curtain-call.
They'll disappear completely.

Music Man

Hamish swings opens his gate
and strolls down Stormy Hill
he's coming for my 58
wrapped up hard against the chill
in his winter hat and coat
Co-op bag in hand
he's a music man of note
says he used to be in a band
you should hear the things he's said
he could've made it big
but loaded the van instead
as a roadie, for Runrig.

Hamish still keeps in touch
with the lads from the band
Donnie still lives on Skye
he's got a nice piece of land
Hamish still plays sessions
but things never go as they should
but at least he's become famous
in his local neighbourhood
you should hear the things he's said
he could've made it big
but made the coffee instead
for his mates, in Runrig.

Aye, that'll be Hamish then
he's always in demand
has a recording studio in his shed
says he now manages a band
he says they're gonna go on tour
he once showed me a pic
'Have you heard of them before?'
I said 'they look a bit like Runrig'

you should hear the things he's said
he could've made it big
but lugged the kit from gig to gig
as a roadie, for Runrig.

Time Machine

If I had a time machine, I'd travel to Paris, 1874
assuming I could go back to a time before I was born.
I'd visit the first Impressionists Exhibition, see it first hand
and mingle with Monet, Degas, Renoir, and Cezanne.
I'd look at the paintings for sure, the oils still wet
at the greatness around me, unrecognized as yet.

But more than that I'd listen to their chatter
I don't understand French but that wouldn't matter.
Critics wrote "worse than wallpaper in its embryonic state."
I'd want to tell the artists to be patient, to just wait.
But they wouldn't need me those Impressionist dudes
instead, I'd investigate other historical interludes.

Search out Robin Hood, witness the fall of Rome
go and find out who built those mighty pyramids of stone.
The thing is no one would listen to a word I say
upon my return they'd not give me the time of day.
The experts would dismiss any evidence I brought
if it interfered with what they already thought.

Perhaps though with more focus on the seminal detailing
I could stop evil taking hold and prevailing
sink the Nina, the Pinta and the Santa María
then send Mr. Columbus off with a flea in his ear.
I could stamp out the Great Fire of London before it took hold
but maybe such things are just meant to unfold.

Alternatively, I could check out the future instead
assuming I could go forward to times when I'm dead.
Is what we're fighting for worth the pain?
Are the efforts and hardships for some future gain?
It's essential to believe that to be true
it's what drives us on, what gets us through.

I guess it would be nice to see some confirmation
it's frustrating having things left to imagination.

Review all I'd known and loved, all I'd despised
perhaps even witness my own demise.
How would that really make me feel inside
when it's laid out before you and there's nowhere to hide?
Would I be able to make sufficient sacrifice
to change a single thing in my life?

Would it make even the slightest difference
to know that the future has a kind of indifference?
I do have a time machine, in the here and the now
it requires I focus on the present to allow
body and mind to sync with life's ebb and flow
to let time's arrow lead me where I need to go.

Coffee Chain Hues

Inspirational quotes
flapjacks and rolled oats
lattes and gingerbread men

sugar rush High Street views
decorated in this year's browns and blues.
Boy, I got the coffee chain hues.

Tarts and savoury bites
take your drinks black or white.
Frappuccino, cappuccino

check out our speciality brews
have you heard the news?
Boy, I got the coffee chain hues.

Our cakes are gorgeous
if you take out a mortgage
lemon drizzle and hot chocolate fudge

put on your comfy shoes
there are endless fucking queues.
Boy, I got the coffee chain hues.

Never

I told her that I loved my version of her.
She told me that she loved
her version of me.

But she never did.

Everything's a hundred percent recyclable
if you wait long enough.
I measure time
on a geological scale
but I'm left trying to read tea leaves
in a coffee cup.

Though it is the most positive
of the negative emotions
I try not to succumb
to the deathly seduction
of regret.
I seek the tiny sweet spot
that sits beside instead.

In Paris, I recall
the hullabaloo
when she got herself a tattoo
of Audrey Tautou
(a busker in the market square
sang in an American accent
while it rained from a clear blue sky)
and later on, she said,
"Let's get pepper sprayed
by the French police.
Let's go and dance naked
up the Champs Elysée."

But we never did.

From here, there and nowhere
it comes again for free
so, take your bagged up dog shit
and tie it to that tree
this form of revisionism
is not for the likes of me.

She told me that she loved her version of me.
I told her that I loved
my version of her.

But I never did.

Mea Culpa

I killed you
but I didn't mean it.
Was I sad
or was I just a coward?
I'm not sure what my mood was,
somewhere between blue and yellow,
a jealous shade of green, perhaps.

Mea culpa
but I don't mean it.
The sun rises later now
and the sky doesn't speak to me.
I'm stuck at the lights,
somewhere between yellow and red,
a fruity shade of orange, perhaps.

I'll go and vote
but I won't mean it.
I'll hold a minute's silence
then spoil my ballot paper.
I'm not sure what the choices are,
somewhere between red and blue,
a regal shade of purple, perhaps.

I killed you
but I didn't mean to.

Last Day

Tomorrow is the day that I die
on the operating table
and I'm stuck in conversation
with an alpha male
both of us with nowhere to go.
Sometimes what doesn't kill you
makes you wish you were dead.

Tomorrow is the day that I die
yet still I have questions.
Why are we so dismissive
of the power of placebo?
And when the fuck did people
start using 'overwhelm'
as a noun?

Town and Country Life

Litter strewn, block-paved wagon trail
Jitterbug-dancing sneakers in the park.
I can still get awfully upset
for someone who doesn't care
that I fail to complete the simplest task.
Can't find a sexagenarian to cut my hair
young barbers round here don't do what you ask.

Shreds of paper feed her daily chronicle.
Extra points for perseverance, not
but with her flaxen cowlick and kinky monocle
I've never seen an iceberg so hot.
She's serving for the match.
I'm in bits, didn't get a trigger warning
didn't get my usual coffee shot this morning.

His brand of racism is particularly nuanced
a mélange of fucked up miscellanea.
According to his wisdom Latvians are fine
but you can't trust those Lithuanians.
Heavy shit with a gravitational pull
that could draw the tide in three hours early
from Zeebrugge to Hull.

But there's no scope to turn my bus around
no hand sanitizer for filthy fingers.
There's a man shouting in the street
but no one's listening, nobody lingers.
The doctors have given him six months to die.
It's been another epic encounter then
best dry my eyes, smile and wave goodbye.

They Bled Gnarled Fingers Dry

The details that were revealed
in his past-life hypnotic regression
were rooted in the earth.
A life of toil as a farmer
in muddy fields of despair
struggling to understand.
Subjugated under the yoke
of avaricious types.
They asset stripped.
They bled gnarled fingers dry.

Scanning a life that's already over.
Bent under leaden skies.
He said he didn't like Helsinki
because he could never find the centre
but Helsinki's like the universe
everywhere's the centre
and if you don't like the universe
no one can help you.
They asset stripped.
They bled gnarled fingers dry.

Pivotal lifetime events
that shape and mould
the emerging soul.
Eighty-six years old
when death lent him a hand.
Terrible injuries, but no pain.
The dead don't feel
only the living.
They asset stripped.
They bled gnarled fingers dry.

Three Choirs Festival

A string quartet on the cathedral green
over Elgar's statue, swooning notes pass
elderly folk sit becalmed and serene
while children turn cartwheels on the grass.

A union flag from a grey sky flares
festival goers with hats and ice cream
finish their sandwiches on plastic chairs
in Hereford, where no one hears you dream.

The Chains of Dogma

All manner of religious bullshit
is preached by the holy seer
from his gilded temple pulpit
cultivating intolerance and fear
while the godless intelligentsia
are rushing headlong to develop
those founts of artificial dementia
they depend on us to envelop.

It's clear that religion and science
have no doctrines to address
the anomaly of that noncompliance
they butt against infinite regress
and it gets worse the harder you look
I'm left drawing sceptical conclusions
it's time to close the opened book
on these virtual reality illusions.

Frictionless Motion

Skye

Remember me to Valtos
on the spume flecked road from Lealt
dinosaur bones and storm tossed
red zinc roofs over peat
to the rain drenched air of Storr
where the Trotternish rocks
descend down Staffin's shore
as gaelic gulls tumble and mock.

Remember me to Glasnakille
on the salt sprayed road from Elgol
to Sligachan and Kyleakin
and beaches of kelp and coral
to the mossy trek up Scorrybreac
atop the Portree brae
that wends from Shullishader Beag
and climbs above the bay.

Remember me.

Portrait

A lonely concerto; flamenco guitar
that shock of fracture can't reunite
Ana sat broken; tears in the bazaar
though we gazed up at the stars that night.

In the Sierra's lustrous fragility
artistic spirits were robed and crowned
through Granada's defiant nobility
illicit dreams were let loose, unbound.

I painted her portrait through May
thick impasto contoured her soul
canvas colour danced an acrylic ballet
to those olive grove moments, we stole.

Now only in self-indulgent reverie
will almond blossom fall once more
conjured from the rubble of memory
over the stones of San Nicolas Mirador.

Frictionless Motion

She was a still-life
in frictionless motion
enchantment underplayed.
How did I draw her attention
and fluke a way out
of my masquerade?

Back in the days when
nothing rhymed with orange
and all was as it seemed
the way out was always in.
She advised me to look first
towards Nature.

I recall her words now
barely whispered:
"Bendita la montaña
y bendito el silencio
que lejos de dar respuestas
calman el fuego de las preguntas."

Solace was found
beyond the foothills
where science and art fuse
to a holy reconciliation.
Was it really only a dream
arriving just in time?

*"Blessed is the mountain
and blessed the silence
that far from giving answers
calm the fire of questions."*

Leave Some Things

Ana, when you left, I paused.
A sweep of the brush ought to do it
or so at least, I thought.
The empty, toppled, bottles of shampoo
strange items of clothing
discarded, abandoned.
An alien landed on the White House lawn.

I am brushing out the flat
but if I get too close
there is a pixelation of detail.
When I'm further away
perspective is gained
and I scan the traces differently.
It's best to leave some things un-swept.

We saved one another, briefly.
A mapped-out plan ought to do it
or so at least, I thought.
Packets of food beyond understanding
pdf docs and movie files
devoured, digested.
I no longer trust what words are for.

I am sweeping out my brain
to tidy space for yours, Ana,
where Lanzarote meets the world.
When you're further away
perspective is lost
but impression comes into focus.
It's best to leave some things un-kempt.

The Day You Died

Abruptly, your spirit called by.
I wore its weary heaviness
my energy and life force draining.
I thought I was dying
the day you died.

Timelines

Memories forged from a chance encounter
timelines that touched, yet two faulted seams.
She radiated a joyous fanfare about her.

Trysts flung on the decks of summer verandas
timelines that kissed, yet in stifled screams.
She radiated the dance of a thousand candles.

In the south of Spain on a whim and a prayer
timelines that withered, yet drank from dreams.
She radiated love to banish my despair.

The Wristwatch

The wristwatch you left behind
has stopped working.
I could never bare to look at it
because each second it ticked off
moved us further apart.
Now that it sleeps
the chasm between us
is unbridgeable.

The Dark Side of the Moon

I remember one time as kids
when we innocently lay on the grass
cloud watching.
I saw one that looked like Africa
and you said,
"What cloud?"
You always were one for
blue sky thinking.

Now Ana my friend you're an astronaut.
Every time you return to earth
there's much catching up to be done
and many cups of tea to be drunk.
My white enamel teapot
reminds me of the chocolate biscuits
you always dunk in my cup
in case the soggy bit breaks off and sinks.

The dark side of the moon
is bathed in sunlight.
We reach the wrong conclusion
just because it's out of sight.
Cloud watching.
Blue sky thinking.
Endless amounts of tea drinking.
Broken-off bits of chocolate biscuits,
sinking.

Meteor Showers

So, I returned to the mother country.
Not even the prospect of clear skies
and the opportunity to wonder
at the Perseid meteor shower could deflect my intentions.
Things had run their course, you see.
The universe has rules that apply here on Earth.
I cracked
and went into the night.
There were no long goodbyes though
because I hate them.
I feel they disempower.

So, two good decisions, consequently.
I heard the meteor shower was shite,
the sky full of thunder.
The move on the other hand, was a spectacular intervention.
Things had run their course, you see.
The universe has rules applied for all they're worth.
I packed
and booked a flight.
There were no long goodbyes though
because I hate them.
More than meteor showers.

Willing Hands No More

See the grain of wood
the nap of flow.
Contemplate the irony of sand
in a glass vessel
pouring into a hollow receptacle.

A dynamic misting
a bullshit meadow of latticed gold
threaded like gossamer braids
adorning the table top mountain
you were always too busy to climb.

Hold onto the pen
to fill the wish of abandonment.
Put your hand inside the mind
and let go
of your questions.

Night skies and larks
in frosted parcels of icing
powder-sugaring the pill of it.
Round the flowing river of mud
cheering the welcoming sun.

The quanta of time
staining the iron bonds
of willing hands no more.
Let them dissolve about you
in shades of varying colours.

Scale the underpass of adventure
do not lose sight of the pen.
The whip hand of fate is at your door
as autumn passes to winter

the dirt of gloaming.

Keep moving into the firmament
of hallowed mantle
and wattled structure
Don't stop now!
There is no termination of life.

This Life

Time travel's possible
though time itself is an illusion.
The space between is where the action is.
Spatially aspirational liberated souls
melted into Earth.

But I'll tell you something else;
6EQUJ5 - the *Wow! Signal*
brave, but wrong.
"Sorry, we're closed
due to shortage of staff."

You don't have to do anything in this life
because
you already do it.

Theta wave gong baths; shamanic meditation.
People rarely donate pairs of socks
to the homeless.
A bald man in the sweltering sun.
The moss on the roof
holds the slates in place.

What if it's all a dream
in the mind of a woman
with a unibrow?

It's not all good but it's not all sad.

You don't have to be anything in this life
because
you already are it.

Note: *The Search for Extra-terrestrial Intelligence (SETI) recorded what became known as the 'Wow! Signal' in August 1977. The six characters on the computer printout, 6EQUJ5, represented a strange and as yet unexplained anomaly. The signal originated from the constellation Sagittarius*. It has never been detected since.*

Perhaps in our ceaseless search for life elsewhere in the universe we sometimes forget to look more deeply at the life we have been gifted on Earth.

*Ana was Sagittarian.

Ana Quintana Carrasco
1988 – 2021

Other Works by Derek Dohren

Wasp in My Cockpit - Black Eyes Publishing UK, 2020
ISBN-13 978-1913195137

Everything Rhymes with Orange - Black Eyes Publishing UK, 2019
ISBN-13 978-1913195038

The Cats of the River Darro - CreateSpace Publishing, 2012
ISBN-13 978-1478315537

Ghost on the Wall (The authorised biography of former Liverpool FC player and manager Roy Evans) - Mainstream Publishing, 2004
ISBN-13 978-1840188325

* * *

Awarded Landscape Artist of the Year 2009 by Artists and Illustrators Magazine for his painting
'The Fossil Hunters'

Derek's artwork can be viewed at
www.derekdohren.com

Testimonials

A beautiful, beguiling collection from a poet unafraid to navigate his way through the gentleness and turbulence of beginnings and endings - of life, death and everything in between. Ranging in scope from cosmic considerations to waiting for the gas man, Dohren deftly explores the interconnectivity of surreal and mundane elements that make up human existence. A bus driver, Dohren uses his experiences and observations as compelling metaphors to reflect intensely on the mechanisms and effects of time, and the business and purpose of living - and dying.

Dohren revels in the frivolity and playfulness of language, and his unexpected turn of phrase provides much satisfying joy. Refrains and repetitions sneak cunningly into poems, patterns are followed and disrupted, deadpan details become a cause for celebration. *Frictionless Motion* is split into two sections, but the personal 'soul connection' between the poet and his deceased friend Ana, shines brightly over the whole collection. For Dohren, 'time's not linear' and his journeys into the human psyche and his relationship with Ana take us round many hairpin bends. But despite the obstacles (that we are told are not all good but not all sad), ultimately we are left with a sense of profound fulfilment as we reach the final words of the closing poem: 'You don't have to be anything in this life/because/you already are it.' *Frictionless Motion* makes an ideal travelling companion when exploring this world and, perhaps, those beyond.

Sara-Jane Arbury, writer, poet, performer, tutor

""Being human's a tough gig" writes Derek Dohren in this, his 3rd poetry collection. It is a book of two halves woven throughout with Derek's unique voice and a fascination with the metaphysical.
In the first half he takes a look at our world and our lives from unexpected angles - from the mundane to the mad, from the light to the profound, from the tiniest detail to universal ponderings, from the melancholy to the hilarious.
In the second, the toughness of that human gig comes to the fore as he produces his most personal work yet, dealing with the love for someone precious but lost.
Frictionless Motion is both excellent and intriguing. It will linger with you."

Chloë Jacquet slam champion and award-winning spoken word poet

From the mind space of a bus cockpit, driving passengers in Gloucestershire and beyond, the everyday and global are examined in this often-surreal take on one man's journey, as he navigates both his scheduled route and a life which may have 'diversions in place'.

Zak D. Dicks, Gloucestershire Poet Laureate, founder and director of Gloucester Poetry Festival

This is a lovely collection. Moving, thought-provoking and entertaining on the page, and with the wit and humour that you always get from Derek's live performances. I wish I'd known Ana.

Colin Wells, multiple poetry slam winner.

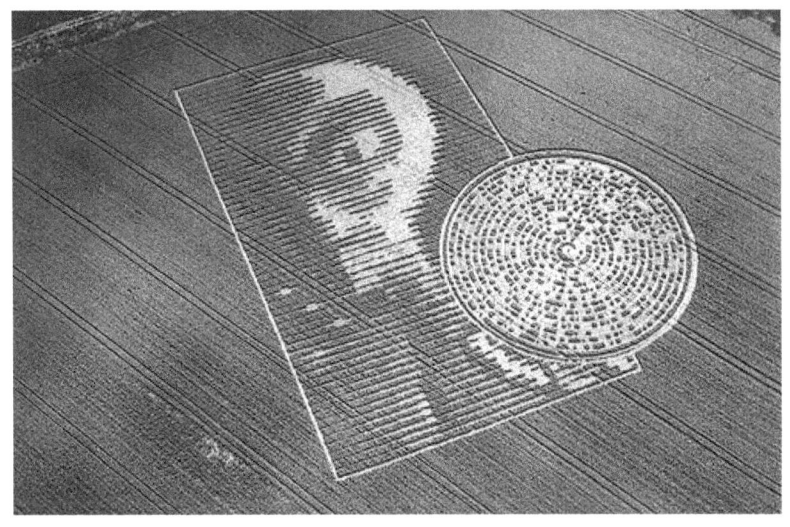

Crabwood crop circle, August 2002.

The Wow! Signal, August 1977.

www.ingramcontent.com/pod-product-compliance
Lightning Source LLC
Chambersburg PA
CBHW041309110526
44590CB00028B/4307